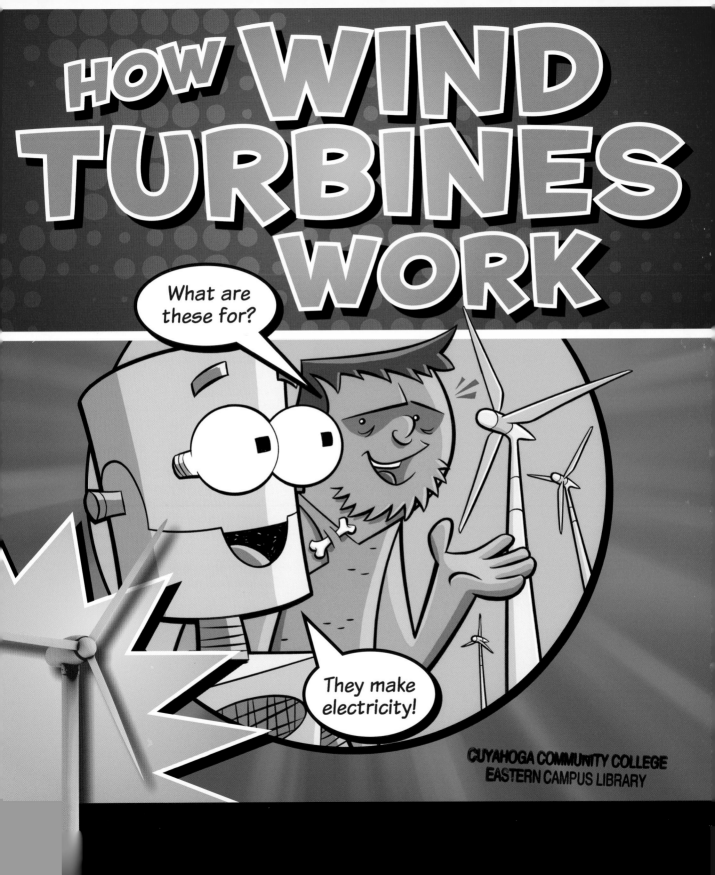

The Child's World®

Published by The Child's World®
1980 Lookout Drive • Mankato, MN 56003-1705
800-599-READ • www.childsworld.com

ACKNOWLEDGMENTS
The Child's World®: Mary Berendes, Publishing Director
Content Consultant: Paul Ohmann, PhD, Associate Professor
  of Physics, University of St. Thomas
The Design Lab: Design and production
Red Line Editorial: Editorial direction

LIBRARY OF CONGRESS
CATALOGING-IN-PUBLICATION DATA
Jacobson, Ryan.
 How wind turbines work / by Ryan Jacobson;
illustrated by Glen Mullaly.
     p. cm.
 Includes bibliographical references and index.
 ISBN 978-1-60973-224-0 (library reinforced: alk. paper)
1. Wind turbines—Juvenile literature. I. Mullaly, Glen, 1968– ill.
II. Title.
 TJ828.J33 2011
 621.31'2136—dc23   2011013789

Photo Credits: Spectral-Design/iStockphoto, cover, 1,
9 (right), 31; iStockphoto, 6 (left), 7 (top), 26, 27; Guy
Erwood/Shutterstock Images, 9 (middle); Craig Wactor/
Shutterstock Images, 11; Bill McKelvie/Shutterstock Images,
18; Shutterstock Images, 21; Library of Congress, 6 (right), 7
(bottom); Alfred T. Palmer/Library of Congress, 8; Paul Fleet/
iStockphoto, 9 (left)

Printed in the United States of America in Mankato,
Minnesota.
July 2011
PA02092

ABOUT THE AUTHOR
Ryan Jacobson is a successful author and presenter. He has written nearly 20 children's books—including picture books, graphic novels, chapter books and choose-your-path books—with several more projects in the works. He has presented at dozens of schools, organizations, and special events. Ryan lives in Mora, Minnesota, with his wife Lora, sons Jonah and Lucas, and dog Boo. For more about the author, please visit his website at www.RyanJacobsonOnline.com.

ABOUT THE ILLUSTRATOR
Glen Mullaly draws neato pictures for kids of all ages from his swanky studio on the west coast of Canada. He lives with his awesomely understanding wife and their spectacularly indifferent cat. Glen loves old books, magazines, and cartoons, and someday wants to illustrate a book on How Monsters Work!

TABLE OF CONTENTS

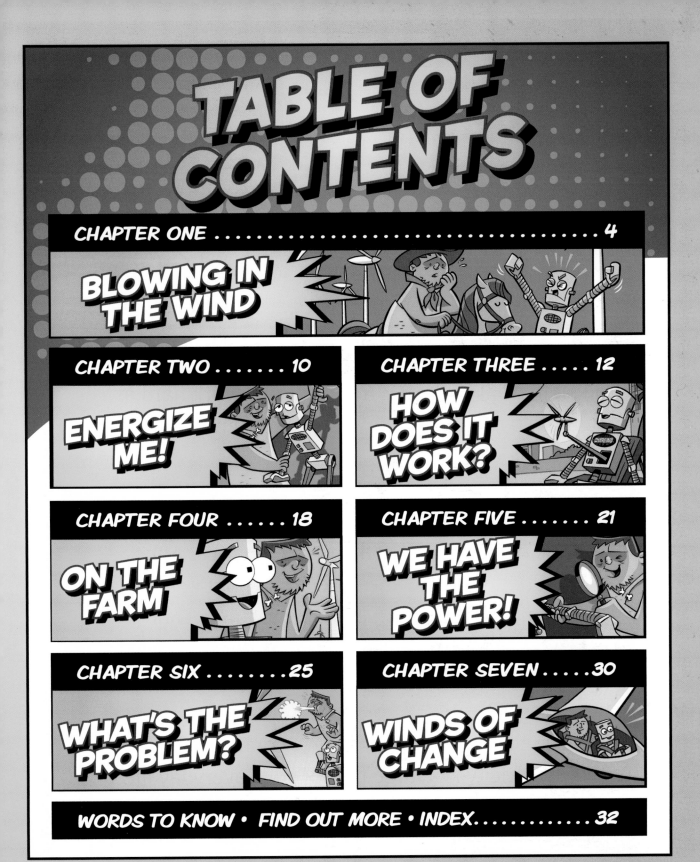

CHAPTER ONE

BLOWING IN THE WIND

You sit in front of the TV. Your thumbs work hard as you try to pass the fifth level of your Mummy Surfer video game.

Suddenly, your mom calls, "Sweetie Pie, it's time for homework."

Game over. You turn off your electronics. After all, you don't want to waste electricity. But here's a question. Do you need electricity to finish your homework? Before you answer, consider this: Is your homework on the computer? Are the lights turned on? Is your room heated . . . or maybe cooled?

Well, you're not a caveman. Of course, the answer is "yes." Electricity is a large part of your everyday life.

We get electricity from all sorts of different places—including the wind. Believe it or not, wind is full of energy. In fact, people have used wind energy throughout history. After all, how did the pilgrims sail to America? Their ships were pushed by wind energy!

Let's take a quick look at wind energy over the years.

30 YEARS AGO

The United States and other countries counted on oil for energy. But the amount of oil needed was far greater than what was available. Plus, oil became very expensive. People wanted cheaper energy options— such as wind energy. Countries in Europe and North America started building bigger and better wind turbines. Some places built large groups of wind turbines, or wind farms. These could collect and store even more wind energy.

> I said WIND farm!

TIME LINE

ABOUT 5000 BC
Egyptians begin using wind power to sail along the Nile River.

ABOUT 200 BC
Simple windmills are used in China and the Middle East to pump water and grind grain.

ABOUT 800 AD
Arab sailors invent the lateen sail. It can catch wind from almost any direction.

ABOUT 1100 AD
Europeans begin using windmills.

100 YEARS AGO Electric lights, toasters, and vacuums were new household inventions. But there was no electric company and no power lines to make them work. Instead, people's homes were powered by windmills. The windmills produced just enough energy to make a few lights and small appliances work.

1,000 YEARS AGO The world's first windmills had already been invented in Asia. Now they were being built throughout Europe. People used windmills mainly for pumping water and grinding grain.

MID-1800s
The use of windmills spreads across North America.

1870
Steel blades replace wooden blades, making windmills much more efficient.

1888
Charles F. Brush builds the first large windmill. It generates electricity for the city of Cleveland, Ohio.

BY 1890
Larger windmills called wind turbines are built in Denmark.

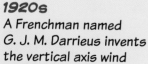

BACK TO TODAY

Oil prices continue to rise, and saving our natural resources is a big concern. So wind energy is more popular than ever. It promises to provide clean energy that will never run out.

THE NUMBERS

Total number of homes in the United States: 130 million

Wind energy produced worldwide: Enough for 6 million homes

Wind energy produced in the United States: Enough for 2 million homes

Wind energy that could be produced in the United States by 2020: Enough for 25 million homes

25 MILLION HOMES BY 2020

1920s
A Frenchman named G. J. M. Darrieus invents the vertical axis wind turbine (the kind that looks like an eggbeater).

BY 1930
Around 600,000 windmills supply electricity and pump water to homes across the United States.

BY 1936
Electric power has been brought to most of the United States.

1941
The world's largest wind turbine is built on a mountain in Vermont.

THAT'S NOT FOR BAKING A CAKE

Wind turbines come in two basic types. The most common looks like an old-fashioned windmill. It usually has two or three blades that spin around an upright pole.

The other type looks more like something you'd use to stir cake batter! It has two or three blades that connect to the top and bottom of a large, upright pole. With the pole, each form a shape similar to the letter D.

This type of turbine catches wind no matter which way it's blowing. But it makes less electricity than the more familiar windmill type. The arched blades are closer to the ground, so wind can be blocked by trees, hills, your brother's big head, and other things.

BY 1945
The United States and other countries rely on coal and other fossil fuels for their energy needs. Wind energy is almost forgotten.

1973
A sharp rise in oil prices sparks new interest in wind energy.

1980s
Countries in Europe and North America build bigger, more efficient wind turbines. Wind farms start to appear.

TODAY
Wind energy is less expensive than ever before. It is the fastest-growing source of electricity in the world.

CHAPTER TWO

ENERGIZE ME!

Energy is a part of everything we are and everything we do. It takes energy to breathe, to walk, to run, to call your sister names, and even to sleep. Energy makes cars go, keeps our houses at just the right temperature, and washes our dirty underwear.

Of course, there are many different types of energy. The energy that keeps your heart pumping isn't the kind that will warm your macaroni and cheese. For hot noodles, you need energy to be changed into electricity.

Lucky for us, wind is a type of energy called **kinetic energy**. Wind turbines turn wind energy into electricity.

Now spin your arms.

I wish I were a toaster.

POWER HOUR!

The price of energy is measured in a unit called a kilowatt-hour (kWh). Sure, it sounds like a fancy word, but a kilowatt equals 1,000 **watts**. An hour is, well, hopefully you know. So a kilowatt-hour means 1,000 watts of power used for an hour. We can figure out the cost of energy by looking at the price of one kilowatt-hour.

Here are some current energy costs:
- Hydroelectric energy (from water): 2–5 cents
- Nuclear energy: 3–4 cents
- Coal energy: 4–5 cents
- Natural gas: 4–5 cents
- Wind energy: 4–10 cents
- Geothermal energy (from the heat of Earth): 5–8 cents
- Biomass energy (from corn or other crops): 8–12 cents
- Solar energy: 15–32 cents

Wind energy is right in the middle. But as wind turbines get better and better, the costs keep going down.

CHAPTER THREE

HOW DOES IT WORK?

WHERE DOES WIND COME FROM?

1. Wind comes from solar energy. That means wind is created by the sun. It all starts when the sun heats a certain area of land. The heated land then warms the air around it.

2. As the air gets hotter, it rises, leaving some room where it used to be.

3. Cold air rushes in to fill that space (kind of like when you race to steal your sister's spot on the couch). This moving air becomes wind.

All right, so wind energy is the wave of the future. But how does a breeze help you watch TV, listen to music, or text your best friend? Where does the electricity come from? First, it might help to find out where wind comes from.

Have you ever flown a kite or ridden in a sailboat? Then you've captured wind for your own use. Wind turbines work in much the same way.

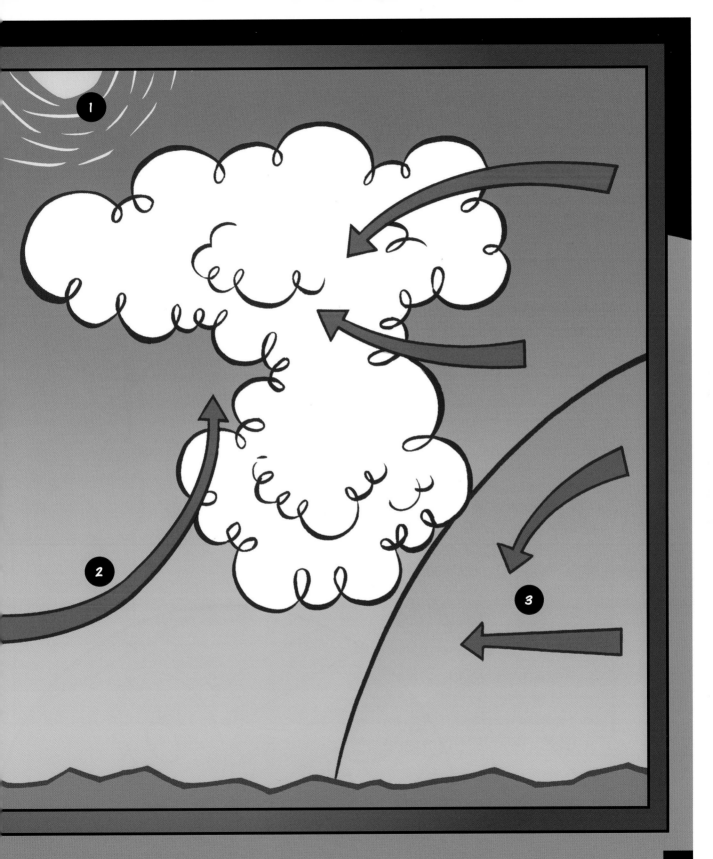

WIND TURBINE

1. Wind pushes the blades of a wind turbine, making them turn. The blades are shaped like airplane wings. They are designed and positioned to catch enough wind so they will turn.

2. The blades connect to a pole, called the main shaft. As the blades spin, the main shaft spins, too.

3. The main shaft leads into a gearbox. Here, there are two gears, a larger one and a smaller one. The main shaft is connected to a larger gear. As the larger gear slowly turns, it makes the second, smaller gear turn beside it. Because this second gear is smaller, it turns more quickly.

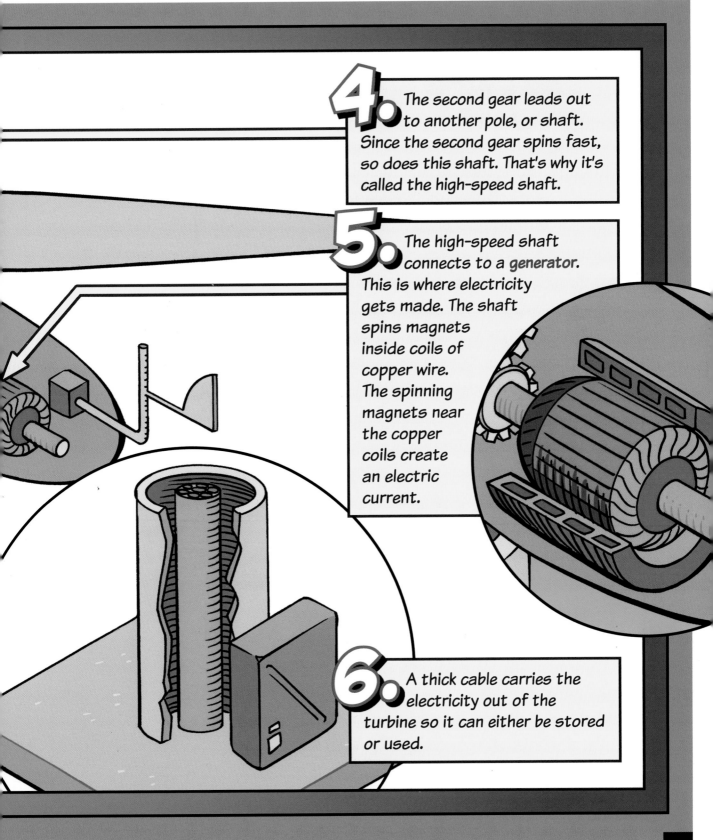

4. The second gear leads out to another pole, or shaft. Since the second gear spins fast, so does this shaft. That's why it's called the high-speed shaft.

5. The high-speed shaft connects to a *generator*. This is where electricity gets made. The shaft spins magnets inside coils of copper wire. The spinning magnets near the copper coils create an electric current.

6. A thick cable carries the electricity out of the turbine so it can either be stored or used.

IT'S NOT MAGIC

Energy exists all around us—and within us. Energy cannot be created or lost. It can only be changed from one form to another. Wind turbines do not create electricity out of nothing. (That would be magic!) They use the wind's kinetic energy, changing it into a form we can use.

TOO MUCH OF A GOOD THING

The more wind the better, right? Wrong! Strong winds can make a turbine's blades spin too fast, which could break them. Luckily, there's a solution for that. When winds become too strong, the blades automatically tilt to catch less wind. Or they shut down altogether.

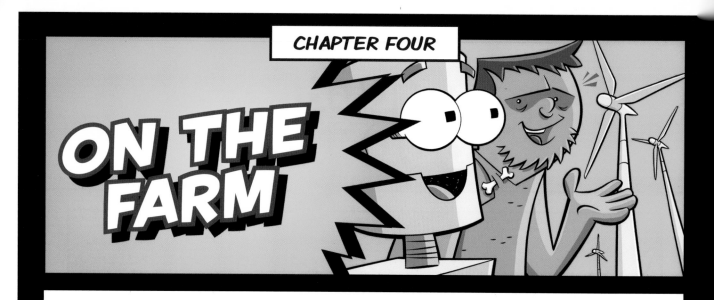

CHAPTER FOUR

ON THE FARM

You've heard of dairy farms, pig farms, and horse farms—but did you know people farm the wind? When several wind turbines are placed together on the same area of land, it's called a wind farm. These groups of turbines work together to make large amounts of electricity.

A single wind farm can have dozens of turbines.

It is especially important for wind farms to be built in places that are—you guessed it—windy. Strong, steady winds are preferred. Some of the best places for wind farms include shorelines, hilltops, areas between mountains, and open fields.

But even on the perfect spot, wind turbines need to be placed in a special way. They can't be too close together. That could make them block each other's wind. But if they're too far apart, then space is being wasted.

So wind farmers have come up with just the right distance. Imagine what spinning blades look like. They make a circle, don't they? First, wind farmers measure across this circle. Then they multiply this number by about seven times. Let's say the distance across the circle is 200 feet (61 m). Then the math would go: 200 x 7 = 1,400. That means the best distance between wind turbines is 1,400 feet (427 m). Of course, this number changes depending on how long the turbines' blades are.

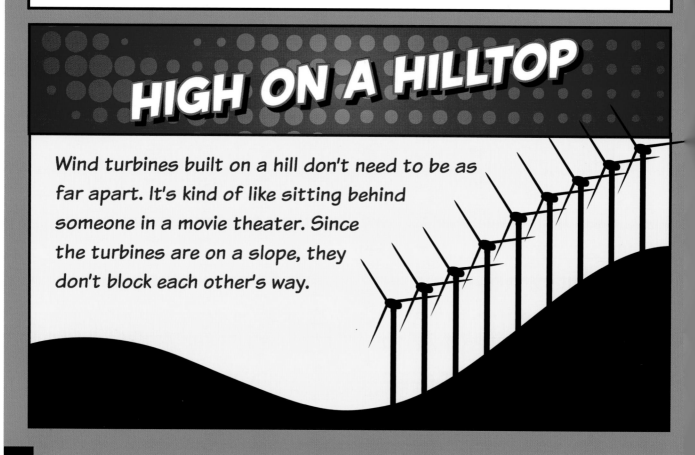

HIGH ON A HILLTOP

Wind turbines built on a hill don't need to be as far apart. It's kind of like sitting behind someone in a movie theater. Since the turbines are on a slope, they don't block each other's way.

CHAPTER FIVE

WE HAVE THE POWER!

So what happens with all of this electricity? Where does wind energy go? The simple answer is that the electric current travels to a **power grid**. From there, it's sent wherever it's needed: homes, schools, your favorite pizza place, you name it.

Of course, if we take a closer look, we'll see that it's a bit more complicated.

Huge pylons support wires that carry electricity into cities.

SUPPLYING POWER

1. Electricity from a wind turbine flows through underground wires to a substation.

2. At the substation, a *transformer* is used to give the electricity a higher *voltage*.

3. A high voltage allows electricity to travel more easily along power lines.

4. Before the electricity flows into a home or building, another substation with another transformer changes the electricity back to a lower voltage. The lower-voltage electricity is now in a usable form.

5. The electricity flows through power lines into neighborhoods and cities. These lines can be aboveground or underground.

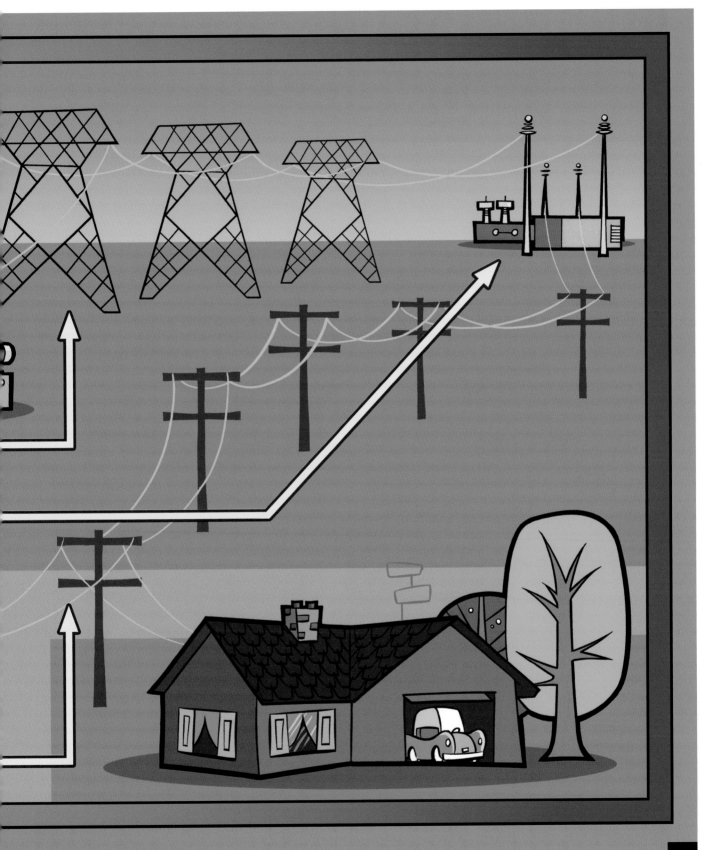

POWERED UP

Power is the rate at which energy is used. Electric power is measured in watts. You can tell how quickly an appliance uses electricity by measuring its wattage. Take a look at the wattage of these household items:

- Clock: 3 watts
- Computer: 365 watts
- Refrigerator: 450 watts
- Hair dryer: 1,000 watts
- Microwave: 1,500 watts
- Air conditioner: 4,500 watts

CHAPTER SIX

WHAT'S THE PROBLEM?

When most people think of energy sources, they don't think of wind energy. That's because **fossil fuels**—coal, natural gas, and oil—are the most used energy sources. Most power plants burn fossil fuels to make electricity. They power our cars and heat our homes. But fossil fuels come with two major drawbacks:

1. Harms Earth

Burning fossil fuels gives off harmful gases.

In 2009, oil, coal, and natural gas supplied almost 80 percent of the energy used in the United States.

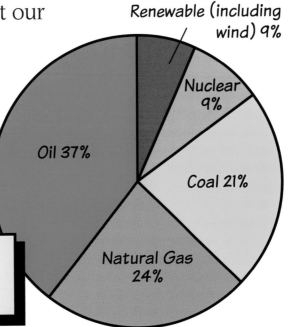

Renewable (including wind) 9%

Nuclear 9%

Oil 37%

Coal 21%

Natural Gas 24%

This air pollution has been known to harm plants and trees, lakes and rivers, and wild animals.

Another result of these harmful gases is that they trap the sun's heat in our atmosphere. This can cause the temperature to rise around the planet. Maybe that doesn't sound so bad at first. After all, who wouldn't want to go swimming every day of the year? But **global warming** could result in all sorts of disasters, such as floods, tornadoes, hurricanes, and more.

Coal-burning power plants are a huge contributor to global warming.

2. Limited Supply

The other downside of fossil fuels is that they will eventually run out. Of course, no one knows when the world's coal, natural gas, and oil will disappear—but it might happen by the time you're a grandparent. Some scientists believe we'll run out of oil in about 40 years and natural gas in about 70 years. Coal will probably last longer, but that could be gone within 250 years.

Wind to the Rescue!

Never fear . . . wind energy is here! And it's got more advantages than your bedroom floor has dirty socks.

1. Wind energy is a "clean" fuel source. That means it doesn't cause pollution when we use it.
2. Wind energy is produced right here in the United States. We don't need to buy it from other countries.
3. Wind energy will never run out. No matter how much we use, we can never use it all up.
4. Wind energy isn't very expensive. In most places, it costs about the same as coal and natural gas.
5. Wind energy is good for farmers. Wind turbines can be built on farmland without taking very much space. The farmers are paid extra money when wind turbines are put on their land.

The Bad News

Unfortunately, wind energy isn't perfect. It does have a downside, too.

1. Wind turbines are expensive to build. Setting up one turbine can cost $80,000.

2. The wind doesn't always blow. People who rely on wind energy also need a backup energy source for those calm, windless days.

3. The windiest places are often far away from where most people live. More power lines are needed to bring the electricity to where it's needed.

4. Flying animals such as birds and bats are sometimes killed when they accidentally fly into the blades of wind turbines.

5. Some people who live near wind turbines complain that the machines are noisy and ugly.

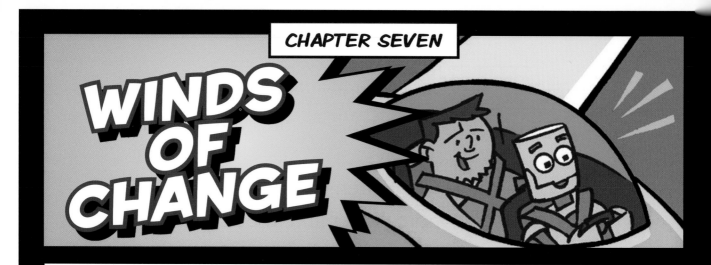

CHAPTER SEVEN

WINDS OF CHANGE

Wind energy could power every home in the United States, but we're not there yet. Right now, wind energy only makes about 1 percent of the power generated in the country.

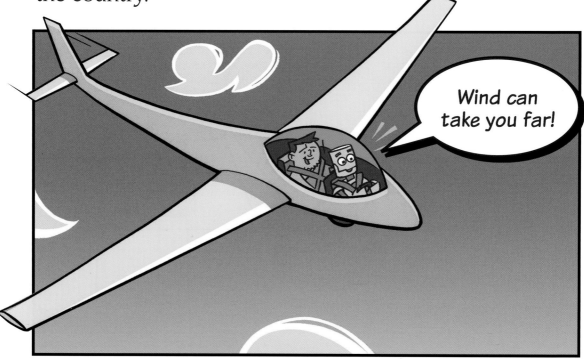

Wind can take you far!

To increase this number, more power grids are needed to connect cities to wind farms. Future wind turbines must work even better than they do today. They must become cheaper to build. All of these things will make wind energy less expensive—and more appealing to those who use it.

Experts around the world are working to improve the way wind turbines work. They are also searching for the best places to build wind farms. With a lot of hard work (and a little luck), who knows how far wind energy will take us?

A BETTER FUTURE? IT'S A BREEZE!

According to the American Wind Energy Association, if we increase our use of wind energy, we will:

- Reduce pollution
- Conserve water
- Lower natural gas prices
- Create more jobs

WORDS TO KNOW

fossil fuels (FOS-uhl FYOO-uhlz): Fossil fuels include oil, coal, and natural gas. Most power plants burn fossil fuels to generate electricity.

generator (JEN-uh-ray-tuhr): A generator is the part of a wind turbine where electricity is generated. Inside a generator, electricity is made by magnets spinning inside coils of copper wire.

global warming (GLOH-buhl WAWRM-ing): Global warming is the increase in Earth's average temperature. Burning fossil fuels causes global warming.

kinetic energy (kih-NET-ik EN-uhr-jee): Kinetic energy is the energy of motion. Wind is a form of kinetic energy.

power grid (POW-uhr GRID): A power grid is a system of cables used to send electric power throughout a region. Electricity from a wind farm travels through the power grid and into homes.

transformer (trans-FOR-muhr): A transformer is a device that changes the voltage of electricity. A transformer increases voltage to allow electricity to travel more easily along a power line or lowers voltage to make electricity safe for home use.

voltage (VOHL-tihj): Voltage is the ability to push electric current. Voltage is increased and decreased by transformers as electricity flows from a wind farm to a house.

watts (WOTS): Watts are units used to measure electric power. Watts measure the rate at which a device uses electricity.

INDEX

FIND OUT MORE

Visit our Web site for links about how wind turbines work: childsworld.com/links

Note to Parents, Teachers, and Librarians: We routinely verify our Web links to make sure they are safe and active sites. So encourage your readers to check them out!